# LOOK AND SEE

## ACTIVITY BOOK

**NATIONAL GEOGRAPHIC LEARNING**

Australia • Brazil • Mexico • Singapore • United Kingdom • United States

**1** TR: 0.1 Listen, point, and say.

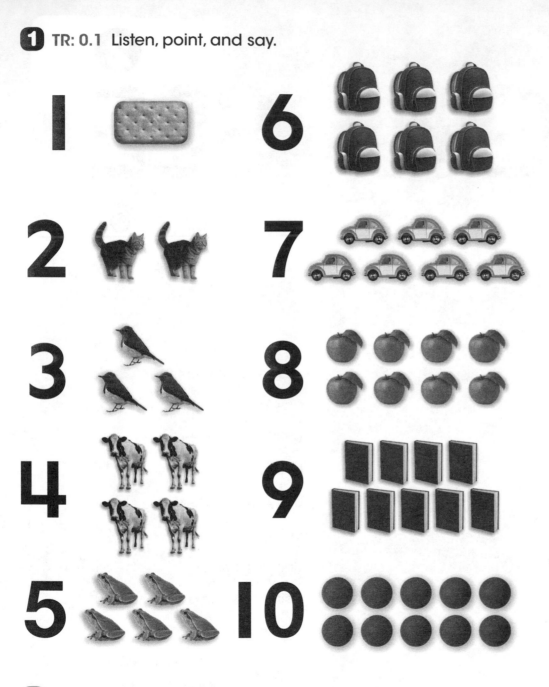

1

2

3

4

5

6

7

8

9

10

**2** TR: 0.2 Listen and chant.

**3** TR: 0.3 Listen, point, and say.

A — ALLIGATOR

E — ELEPHANT

I — IGUANA

O — OCTOPUS

U — UMBRELLABIRD

**1** Draw you. Say.

**1** TR: 1.1 Listen and circle.

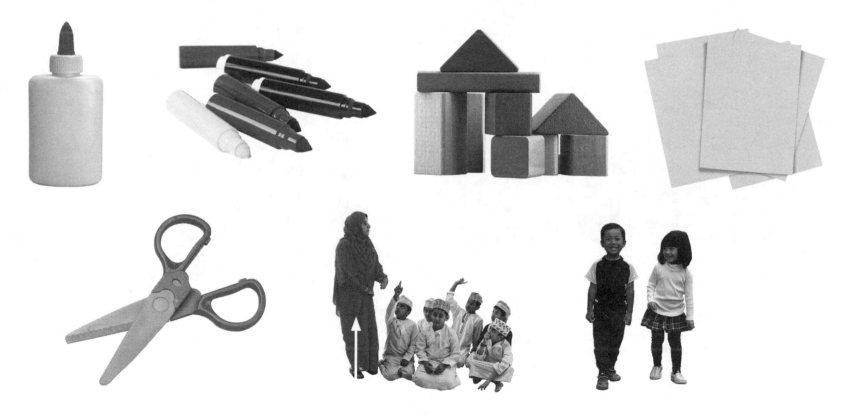

**2** Point and say.

NEW WORDS: *blocks, friend, teacher; glue, markers, paper, scissors*

**1** Draw your family and friends. Then point and say.

**1** TR: 1.2 Circle. Then listen, sing, and point.

**2** Look and circle ✔ or ✘.

VALUE    **BE NEAT IN THE CLASSROOM.**

**1** ✔ ✘

**2** ✔ ✘

**3** ✔ ✘

**1** TR: 1.3 Listen and say.

**B**EAVER

**P**ANDA

**2** Trace.

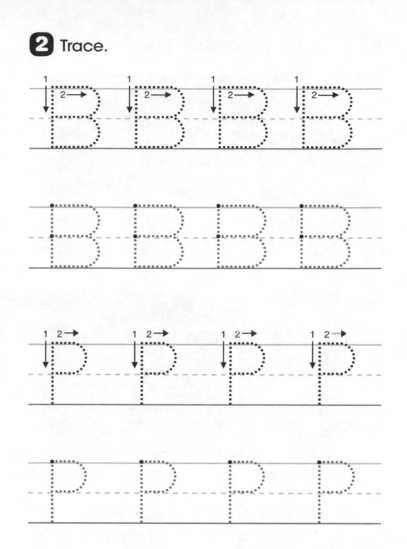

# 1 TR: 1.4 Listen and match.

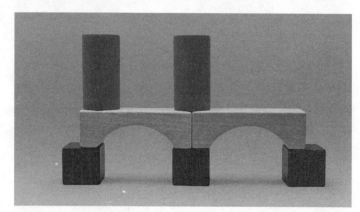

VIDEO: SC: 2 *(optional)*  **Content Words:** *big, bridge, house, small, tower*

**1** TR: 1.5 Listen and point. Then say and color.

REVIEW: **NEW WORDS**: *blocks, friend, teacher; glue, markers, paper, scissors*
**STRUCTURE**: *Who's this? He's my grandpa. She's my friend.*

# 2 ARE YOU HAPPY?

**1** TR: 2.1 Listen. Circle ✔ or ✘.

1 (✔) ✘

2 ✔ ✘

3 ✔ ✘

4 ✔ ✘

5 ✔ ✘

6 ✔ ✘

7 ✔ ✘

**2** Point and say.

**NEW WORDS:** *angry, excited, happy, hungry, sad, sleepy, thirsty*

# 1 Draw you. Then point and say.

**STRUCTURE:** *Are you happy? Yes, I am. Are you sad? No, I'm not.*

11

**1** TR: 2.2 Listen and circle. Then listen, sing, and point.

**2** Look and circle ✔ or ✗.

**VALUE** GET A GOOD NIGHT'S SLEEP.

1 ✔ ✗

2 ✔ ✗

3 ✔ ✗

**1** TR: 2.3 Listen and say.

**2** Trace.

**D**UCK

**T**IGER

**1** TR: 2.4 Listen and match. Then color your favorite.

 1  2 3 4

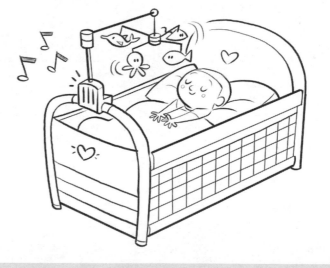

**VIDEO: SC: 4** *(optional)* **Content Words:** *loud, music, quiet*

**1** Play and say.

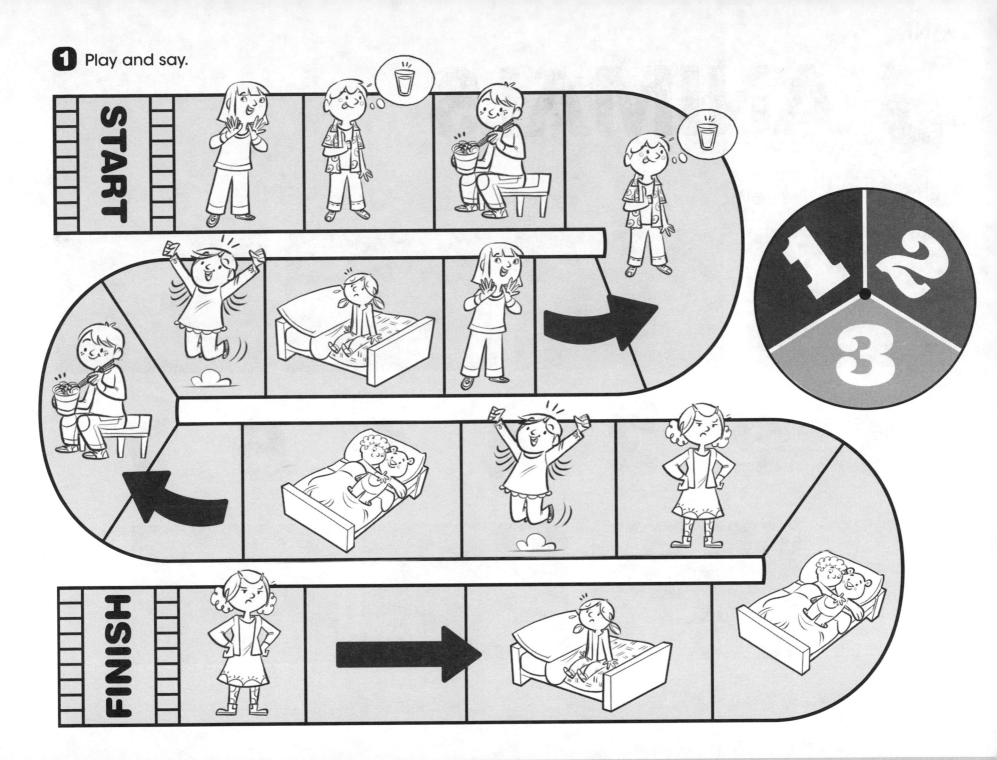

REVIEW: **NEW WORDS**: *angry, excited, happy, hungry, sad, sleepy, thirsty*
**STRUCTURE**: *Are you happy? Yes, I am. Are you sad? No, I'm not.*

15

# 3 ANIMALS

**1** TR: 3.1 Listen and match.

1 2 3 4 5 6 7

**2** Point and say.

**NEW WORDS:** *bat, bear, duck, fox, owl, rabbit, snake*

Match. Then ask and answer.

**STRUCTURE:** *What is it? It's an owl. What are they? They're bears.*

**1** TR: 3.2 Listen and color. Then listen, sing, and point.

**2** Look and circle ✔ or ✗.

**VALUE** BE CURIOUS ABOUT ANIMALS.

**1** ✔ ✗

**2** ✔ ✗

**3** ✔ ✗

**1** TR: 3.3 Listen and say.

S

**S**EAL

Z

**Z**EBRA

**2** Trace.

**1** TR: 3.4 Look and match. Then listen and check.

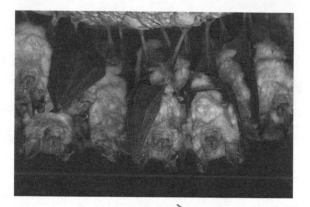

**VIDEO: SC: 6** *(optional)* **Content Words:** *day, night*

**1** Find and color. Then ask and answer.

**REVIEW: NEW WORDS**: *bat, bear, duck, fox, owl, rabbit, snake*
**STRUCTURE**: *What is it? It's an owl. What are they? They're bears.*

21

# 4 GET DRESSED

**1** TR: 4.1 Listen and point.

**2** Point and say.

**NEW WORDS:** *boots, coat, dress, pants, scarf, skirt, sweater*

**1** Draw and color. Then match and say.

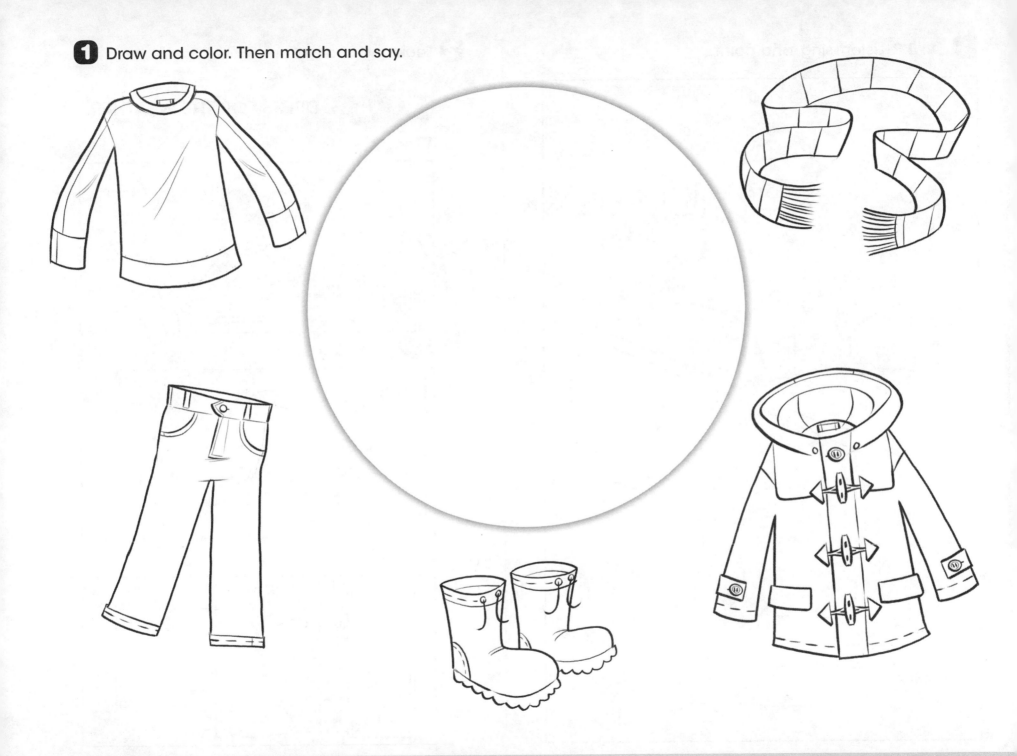

**STRUCTURE:** *This is my sweater. These are my pants.*

23

**1** TR: 4.2 Listen, sing, and point.

**2** Look and circle ✔ or ✘.

**VALUE** DRESS FOR THE WEATHER.

**1** ✔ ✘

**2** ✔ ✘

**3** ✔ ✘

TR: 4.3 Listen and say.

LION

REINDEER

2 Trace.

**1** Color. Play and say.

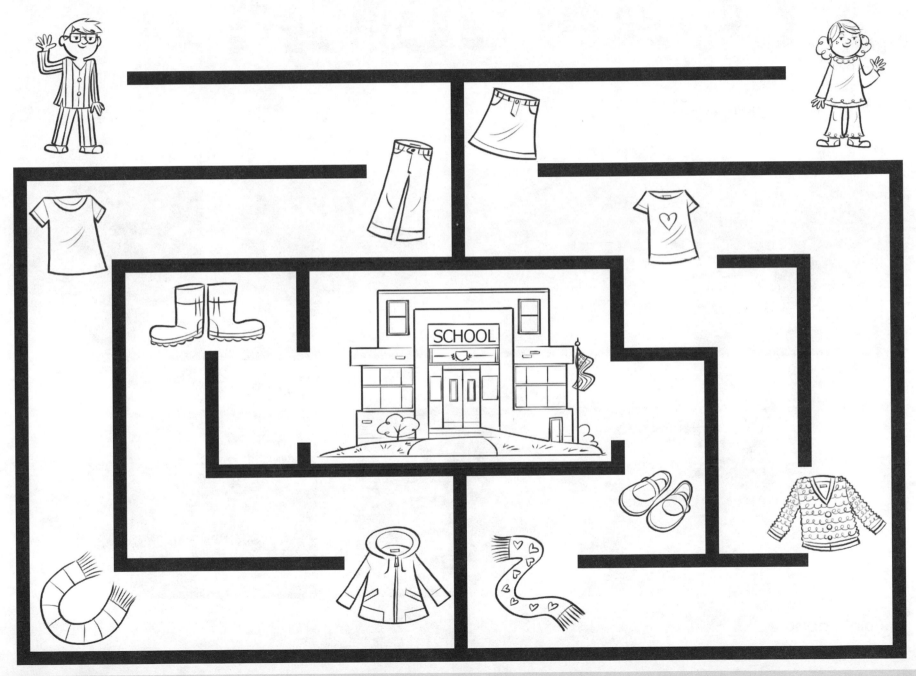

**REVIEW: NEW WORDS**: *boots, coat, dress, pants, scarf, skirt, sweater*
**STRUCTURE**: *This is my sweater. These are my pants.*

27

**1** TR: 5.1  Listen. Circle ✔ or ✘.

**1** ✔ ✘

**2** ✔ ✘

**3** ✔ ✘

**4** ✔ ✘

**5** ✔ ✘

**6** ✔ ✘

**7** ✔ ✘

**2** Point and say.

**1** Do and say.

**1** TR: 5.2 Listen and point. Then sing and do.

**2** Look and circle ✔ or ✘.

**VALUE**  PLAY OUTSIDE.

**1**  ✔  ✘

**2**  ✔  ✘

**3**  ✔  ✘

**1** TR: 5.3 Listen and say.

**MONKEY**

**NUMBAT**

**2** Trace.

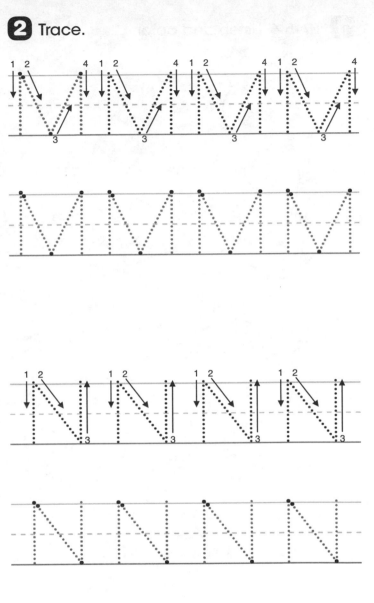

# 1 What can you do? Color, say, and do.

# 6 FACES

**1** TR: 6.1 Listen and point.

**2** TR: 6.2 Listen and draw.

1

2

3

**NEW WORDS:** *ears, eyes, face, hair, mouth, nose; long, short*

**1**  TR: 6.3 Listen. Then draw and color. Say.

**STRUCTURE:** *He has brown eyes. She has long hair.*

**1** TR: 6.4 Listen and color. Then sing and point.

**2** Look and circle ✔ or ✘.

VALUE    SAY NICE THINGS.

1  ✔  ✘

2  ✔  ✘

3  ✔  ✘

# 1 TR: 6.5 Listen and say.

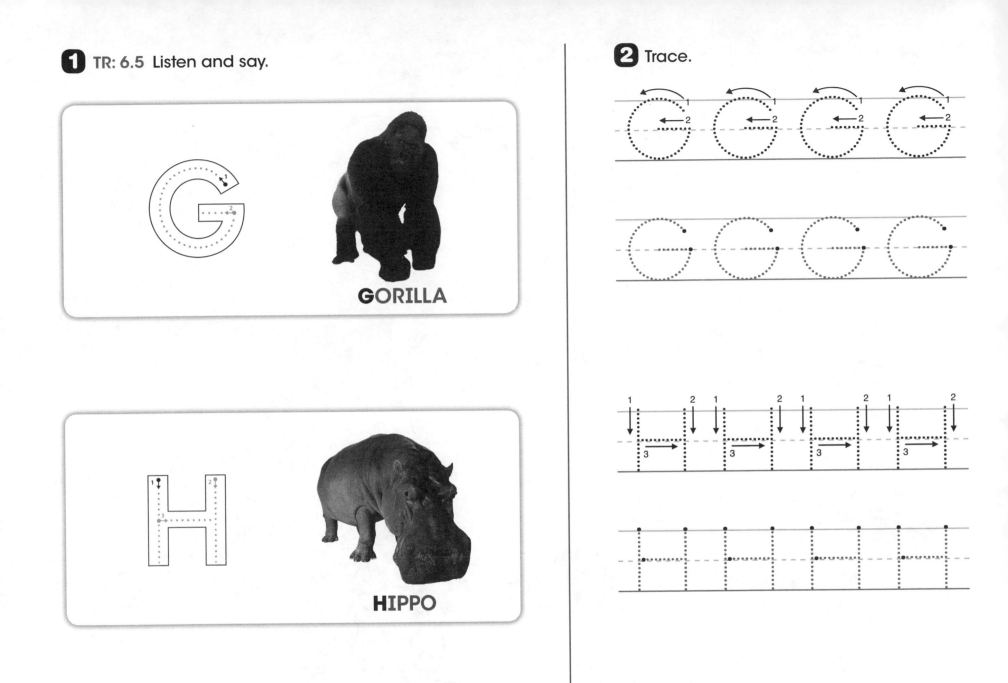

**G**ORILLA

**H**IPPO

# 2 Trace.

# 1 Look and match.

**VIDEO: SC: 12** *(optional)*   **Content Words:** *hear, smell, taste, the senses*

**1** Draw, color, and say.

REVIEW: **NEW WORDS**: *ears, eyes, face, hair, mouth, nose; long, short*
**STRUCTURE**: *He has brown eyes. She has long hair.*

# 7 MY THINGS

**1** TR: 7.1 Listen and match.

1 2 3 4 5 6 7

**2** Point and say.

**NEW WORDS:** *bike, dinosaur, kite, puzzle, robot, scooter, tablet*

**1** Draw one toy. Ask and answer.

**STRUCTURE:** *Is this your kite? Yes, it is./No, it isn't.*

41

**1** TR: 7.2 Listen and circle. Then sing and point.

**2** Look and circle ✔ or ✘.

**VALUE** TAKE TURNS.

**1** ✔ ✘

**2** ✔ ✘

**3** ✔ ✘

**1** TR: 7.3  Listen and say.

**2** Trace.

**CAMEL**

**QUAIL**

**1** Color and count.

**VIDEO: SC: 14** *(optional)*    **Content Words:** *ground, neck, skeleton, tail*

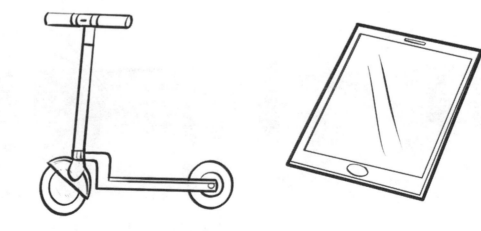

**REVIEW: NEW WORDS**: *bike, dinosaur, kite, puzzle, robot, scooter, tablet*
**STRUCTURE**: *Is this your kite? Yes, it is./No, it isn't.*

# 8 BABIES

**1** TR: 8.1  Listen and match.

**2** TR: 8.2  Listen and point. Then say.

**NEW WORDS:** *baby, calf, chick, kitten, lamb, puppy; big, small*

**STRUCTURE:** *There's one cow. There are two calves.*

**TR: 8.4** Listen and point. Then color.

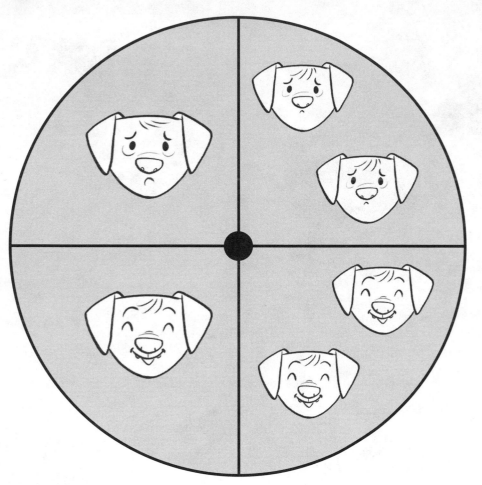

**2** Look and circle ✔ or ✘.

VALUE    BE KIND.

1   ✔   ✘

2   ✔   ✘

3   ✔   ✘

**1** TR: 8.5 Listen and say.

**KANGAROO**

**FOX**

**2** Trace.

**1** Match and say.

**VIDEO: SC: 16** *(optional)* **Content Words:** *ant, egg, ostrich*

**1** Color and say.

REVIEW: **NEW WORDS**: *baby, calf, chick, kitten, lamb, puppy; big, small*
**STRUCTURE**: *There's one cow. There are two calves.*

**1** TR: 9.1 Listen. Circle ✔ or ✗.

**1** ✔ ✗

**2** ✔ ✗

**3** ✔ ✗

**4** ✔ ✗

**5** ✔ ✗

**6** ✔ ✗

**7** ✔ ✗

**8** ✔ ✗

**2** Point and say.
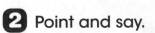

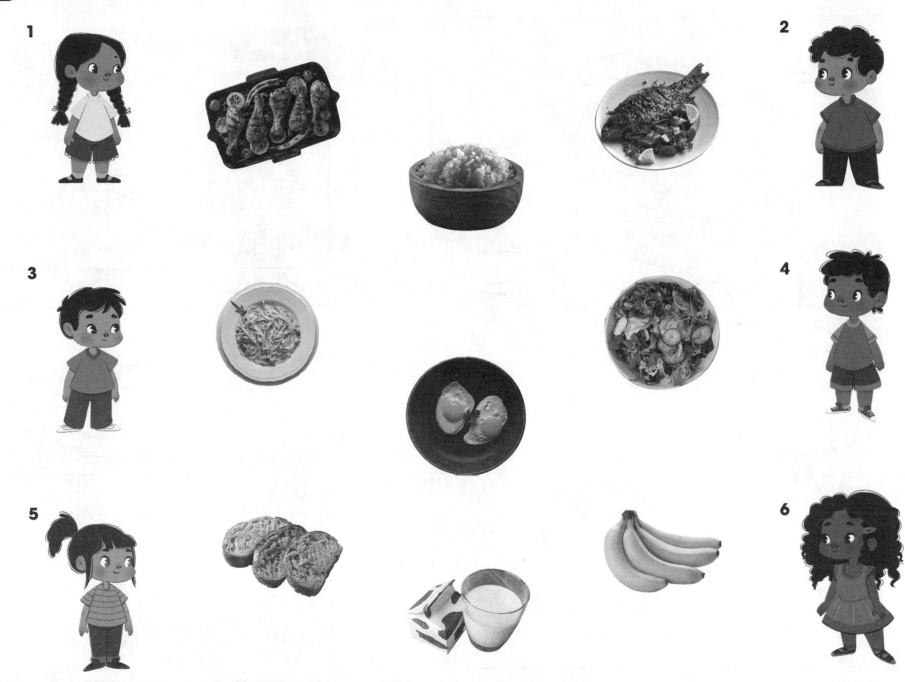

**STRUCTURE:** *What do you want? I want chicken, please.*

**53**

**1** TR: 9.3 Listen and circle. Then color and sing.

**2** Look and circle ✔ or ✗.

1  ✔  ✗

2  ✔  ✗

3  ✔  ✗

**1** TR: 9.4 Listen and say.

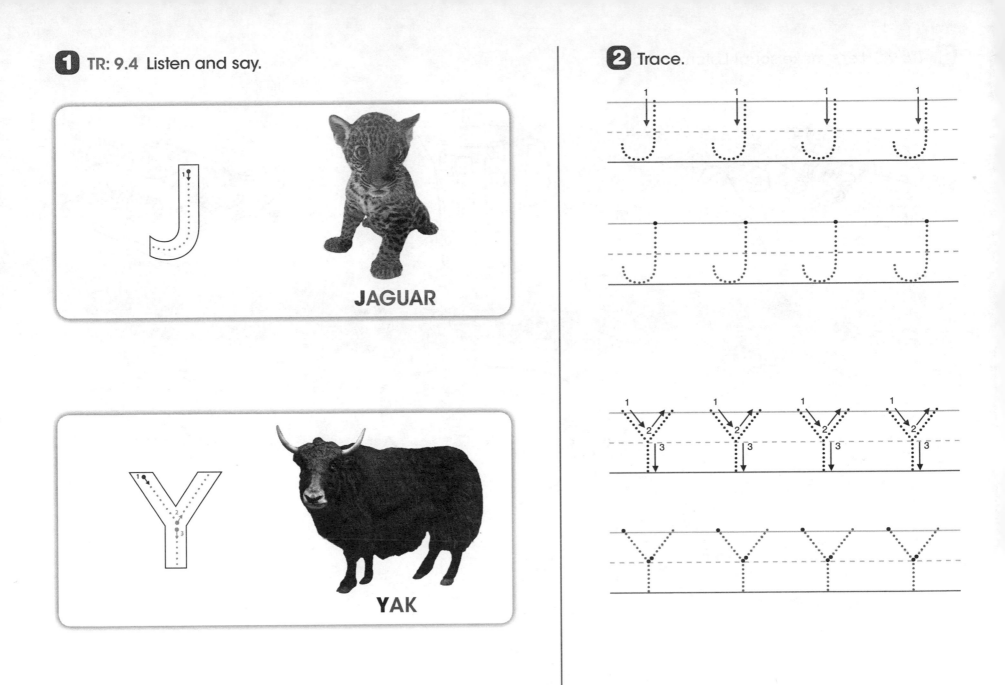

**J**

**JAGUAR**

**Y**

**YAK**

**2** Trace.

**1** TR: 9.5 Let's make soup! Listen and circle.

VIDEO: SC: 18 *(optional)*   **Content Words:** *cook, eat, onion, soup*

**1** What's for dinner? Draw.

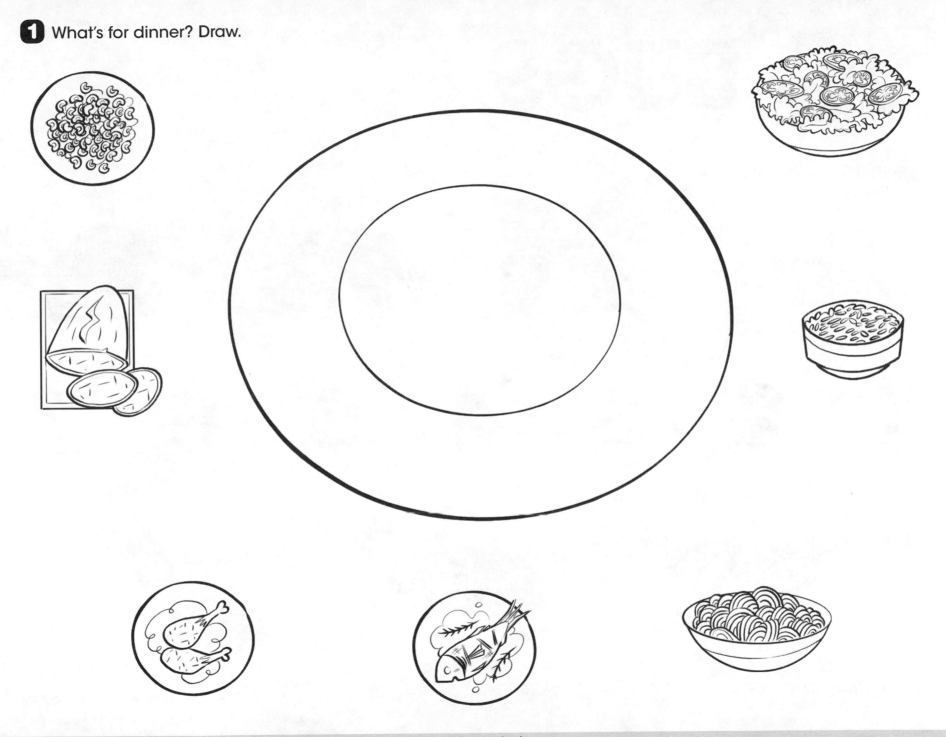

**REVIEW: NEW WORDS**: beans, bread, chicken, dinner, fish, noodles, rice, salad
**STRUCTURE**: What do you want? I want chicken, please.

57

**1** TR: 10.1 Listen and match.

**1**     **2**     **3**     **4**     **5**     **6**     **7**

**2** Look and say.

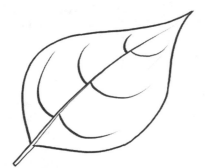

**STRUCTURE:** *Where's the caterpillar? It's on an apple.*

**1** **TR: 10.3** Listen and draw. Then sing and point.

**2** Look and circle ✔ or ✘.

**BE GOOD TO NATURE.**

**1**   ✔   ✘

**2**   ✔   ✘

**3**   ✔   ✘

**1** TR: 10.4 Listen and say.

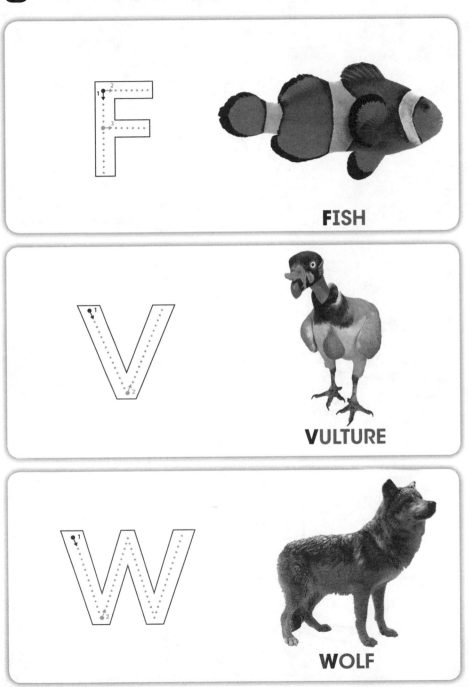

FISH

VULTURE

WOLF

**2** Trace.

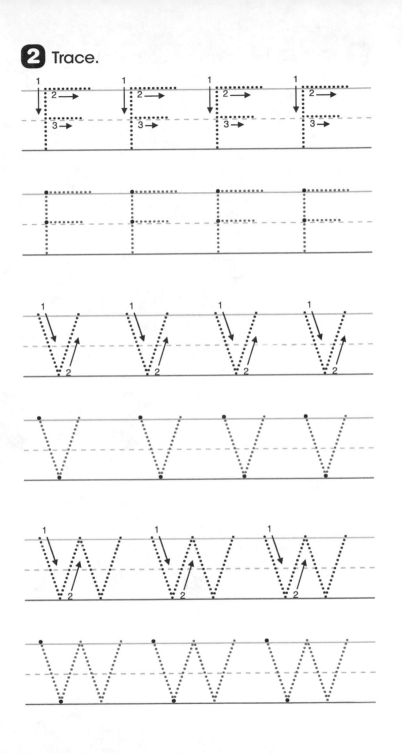

1 TR: 10.5 Listen and match. Color.

**1    2    3    4**

**1** Look and say. Find. Then color.

REVIEW: **NEW WORDS:** *ant, bee, butterfly, caterpillar, ladybug, snail, spider*
**STRUCTURE:** *Where's the caterpillar? It's on an apple.*

63

# CREDITS